GLEN ROCK PUBLIC LIBRARY
GLEN ROCK, N.J. 07452

DOORS TO AMERICA'S PAST

ALAMO:
BATTLE OF HONOR AND FREEDOM

Linda R. Wade

ROURKE ENTERPRISES, INC.
Vero Beach, FL 32964

©1991 Rourke Enterprises, Inc.

All rights reserved. No part of this book may be reproduced or utilized in any form or by any means, electronic or mechanical including photocopying, recording or by any information storage and retrieval system without permission in writing from the publisher.

Library of Congress Cataloging-in-Publication Data

Wade, Linda R.
    Alamo: battle of honor and freedom / by Linda R. Wade.
    p. cm. – (Doors to America's past)

    Includes index.
    Summary: Describes the events surrounding the famous battle in the war for Texan independence.
    ISBN 0-86592-470-8
    1. Alamo (San Antonio, Tex.) – Siege, 1836 – Juvenile literature. 2. Texas – History – Revolution, 1835-1836 – Juvenile literature. [1. Alamo (San Antonio, Tex.) – Siege, 1836. 2. Texas – History – Revolution, 1835-1836.] I. Title II. Series: Wade, Linda R. Doors to America's past.
F390.W15 1991
976.4'03 – dc20
                                                                                                90-46099
                                                                                                    CIP
                                                                                                     AC

Acknowledgments

    Special thanks to the following people, who provided information, pictures and encouragement: Martha Utterback, the Daughters of the Republic of Texas (DRT) Library in the Alamo; Lynn Catalina, Institute of Texan Cultures; Ernest A. Loeffler, Jr., San Antonio Convention and Visitors Bureau; Gale Shiffrin, for her script of the slide presentation, "Texas Under Six Flags"; and Robert E. Hogue, for his editing assistance.

Photo Credits

San Antonio Convention & Visitors Bureau: cover, 12, 32, 34, 36, 37, 42, 43, 45
DRT Library, San Antonio, Texas: 5, 14, 15, 17, 24
The Institute of Texan Cultures: 7
Texas Highways Magazine: 1, 27, 29
Sea World of Texas: 40

Table of Contents

	Introduction	4
1	The Beginnings of San Antonio	6
2	Settlers from the North	10
3	Who Went to the Alamo?	13
4	The Battle of the Alamo	18
5	A Brief Mexican Victory	28
6	San Antonio Today	31
7	A Visit to San Antonio	33
8	A City of Fiestas	41
	Index	47

Introduction

Dead men lay everywhere. And there were more dead men outside the fort than inside. For though the Texans who defended the Alamo were greatly outnumbered, they fought valiantly, delivering stunning blows to the Mexican enemy. The brave freedom fighters never wavered in their cause, Davy Crockett's rifle seldom missed a mark, and when at last the Texans ran out of ammunition, they used their guns as clubs against the invaders.

The year was 1836. Mexico owned most of what is now the southwestern part of the United States, including the Texas territory. Mexico had gained the land in its successful struggle for independence from Spain. But now the Texas frontier people, many of them settlers from the United States, were fearful of Mexico's growing tyranny. They began demanding independence. General Antonio López de Santa Anna, the Mexican president and dictator, saw no choice but to march his forces north to quell the Texans' stirrings of liberty. He set out for San Antonio de Béxar, the capital of the Texas territory.

When he arrived, the ill-prepared Texans withdrew behind the walls of the Alamo, the chapel of an old

Alamo Mission in the early days

Spanish mission that had become a military garrison. What followed was the Battle of the Alamo, a 13-day siege of enormous brutality. But if the bitter struggle meant certain death for all 188 of the defenders, it also gave birth to an even greater spirit of freedom in Texas. It was a spirit that would come back swiftly and sorely to haunt the Mexican leader.

Today, the restored Alamo is a beautiful building in downtown San Antonio, Texas. But let's travel back to the time when it first was a little mission belonging to Spain, then a little fort belonging to Mexico. Let's travel to San Antonio, a city bursting with centuries of history.

1
The Beginnings of San Antonio

The San Antonio River valley has always been a good place to live. Some of the first people to inhabit the area were the Payaya Indians. The valley provided them with a variety of foods to harvest—from pecans to mesquite beans, to the fruit of the prickly pear cactus. The San Antonio River supplied fresh water and fish; and cottonwood trees, plentiful in the area, provided wood to build fires and to cook the game that the Payaya snared.

When the Spaniards arrived in the valley in 1691, Domingo de Téran-Damián Manzanet, the first governor, noted in his diary:

We camped on the banks of a stream adorned by a great stand of trees....I named it San Antonio de Padua because we reached it on his day. Here we found an encampment of the Payaya tribe. We observed their actions, and I concluded that they were docile and affectionate, naturally friendly, and very well disposed toward us....

In 1718, the Spaniards built the San Antonio de Valero Mission. Named for the Marquis of Valero, the viceroy of Mexico, it was one of a growing number of

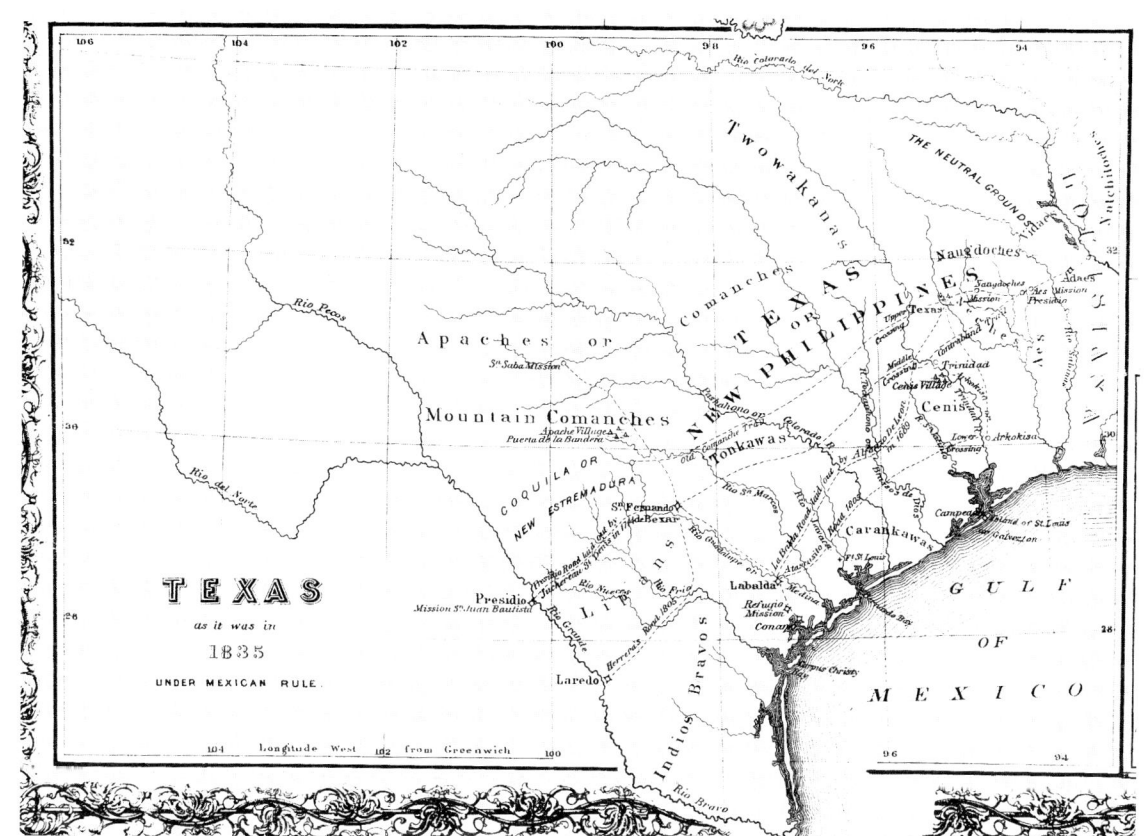

Texas as it was in 1835

missions that the Spanish set up in the New World to bring Christianity to the Native Americans. Built on the San Antonio River, the mission was located on the present site of San Antonio. A town called Béxar (BAR-har) was built around the mission. A fort also was constructed. Called the Presidio de San Antonio de Béxar, the fort was to guard the mission from attacks by Native Americans. The first mission, a compound of crude huts, was, in fact, destroyed, but by a hurricane, not natives. Later buildings crumbled from faulty construction. Finally, in 1758 the mission was replaced by stone buildings that would last longer.

With good reason did the Spanish build forts to protect their missions. For in spite of their efforts, the Spaniards never succeeded in winning over the native people to the Old World way of life. If anything, many natives responded with growing hostility to the white people's moving in on their lands and style of life. During the 1700s, roaming Comanche Indians crossed the plains of Texas, hunting buffalo. They attacked settlements swiftly, looting and killing, then withdrawing quickly. By the late 18th century, conditions had become critical. The governor of San Antonio de Béxar, the capital of the Spanish government in Texas, informed the Spanish viceroy: "There is no instant by day or night when reports of barbarities and disorders do not arrive from the ranches...."

To help the settlers resist the natives, the viceroy sent cavalry to San Antonio de Béxar. When the troops arrived, they moved into the mission, which had by then been abandoned by the church. For one, the priests had failed to domesticate the Native Americans. Then, the few natives who did remain fell victim to an epidemic that killed them off. No longer of religious use, the mission was made a fort by the Spanish and came to be known as the Alamo. The name may have come from Alamo de Parras, the Mexican town from which the cavalry came. The name may also have come from *alamo*, the Spanish word for "cottonwood," trees that grew abundantly around the fort. The Spanish stayed in the fort until Mexican troops took it over from the Spanish in 1821. That was the year Mexico won its independence from Spain. During the years prior to that, revolutionary groups in Mexico had been seeking independence from Spain. One such group of revolutionary fighters swept across the Texas territory, defeating Spanish loyalist forces along the way. The Spanish loyalist soldiers in the Alamo, too, found themselves the target of the revolutionary Mexican troops. One of the young Mexican horse soldiers was Antonio López de Santa Anna, who would later become Mexico's president. His campaign into Texas to rid it of the Spanish would not be his last trip to the northern lands.

2
Settlers from the North

Texas was a vast, wild, and unsettled land in the 1800s. Only three areas were populated: San Antonio de Béxar, the capital of the Texas territory; and the towns of Nacogdoches and of Goliad. All lay in the eastern half of the Texas territory. Because the missions had failed to subdue the natives, the government of the new state of Mexico concluded that settlers were needed in the North to save Texas from the hostile tribes.

With the permission of the Mexican government, Stephen F. Austin and a group of families from the Missouri territory went to Texas in 1821. The colonists were given free land if they promised to obey the laws of Mexico, to become citizens, and to pay taxes after six years. Tempted by the generous offer, other frontier people followed, happily agreeing to the conditions for settling. As news of the bargain spread, more settlers poured into the pleasant open country of mild winters and fertile land.

Though the Mexican government first welcomed the newcomers, problems began to arise when more settlers came than the Mexican government wanted. Some of the settlers defied Mexican law by bringing slaves. Others refused to convert to Catholicism, the religion of the Mexicans. Then the settlers began to demand self-government. Cultural differences in traditions, customs, and language only added to the difficulties between Mexico and the Texas colonists.

In 1833, Stephen Austin traveled to Mexico City to deliver a petition asking President Santa Anna to recognize Texas as a separate state. Austin got an answer quickly: on his way back home, he was arrested on suspicion of inciting a rebellion in Texas and was imprisoned for 18 months. After his release, he was more certain than ever of the course the Texans needed to follow. In September 1835, Austin wrote a letter to his fellow colonists. "War is our only resource," he declared. "There is no other remedy but to defend our rights, our country, and ourselves by force of arms."

Late in 1835, Texas landowners met to discuss their course of action—but the course was decided for them. Santa Anna sent his brother-in-law, General Martín Perfecto de Cos, to San Antonio de Béxar. Cos was to expel all settlers who had come to Texas after 1830 and arrest all Texas patriots who opposed Santa Anna's rule.

Monument honoring the battle heroes and located in the Alamo Plaza

    Arriving in the town, General Cos stationed about 600 troops there and about 600 more in the Alamo. In the meantime, the Texans mobilized, and just before dawn on December 5, 1835, 300 tough and determined volunteers attacked the Mexican troops. A fight, called the Battle of Béxar, raged for three days. By the fourth day, a badly beaten General Cos was forced to surrender. He signed papers giving Texans all the public property, money, arms, and ammunition in the town.

    On Christmas day, the Mexican general and his army, defeated and in shame, returned to Mexico. The blow of having the Mexicans suffer such a stunning defeat at the hands of the colonists was too much for Santa Anna. Now he himself would march his army north and crush the rebellious Texans.

3
Who Went to the Alamo?

Green B. Jameson, a volunteer originally from Kentucky, arrived at the Alamo in early January. Only a few weeks before, he had fought in the Battle of Béxar. He knew that General Cos had left behind lances, bayonets, cannon, and ammunition in the Alamo. If another battle were to take place, he was certain it would be in that fort.

Jim Bowie arrived two weeks later, on January 19. The Kentucky-born adventurer and frontiersman had moved to Texas seven years earlier and was dedicated to the cause of freedom. He had already fought in other early struggles against Mexico. When he heard reports that Santa Anna was planning to march on Texas, he hastened to the Alamo to take command of the volunteers. Since the Alamo was the only outpost between San Antonio de Béxar and the Mexicans, Bowie, too, was sure that any attack made would occur at the fort.

Colonel William Barret Travis arrived at the Alamo on February 3. He was an officer in the Texas colonial army and, with Jim Bowie, was to hold joint command of the Alamo forces. Born in South Carolina and raised in

James Bowie

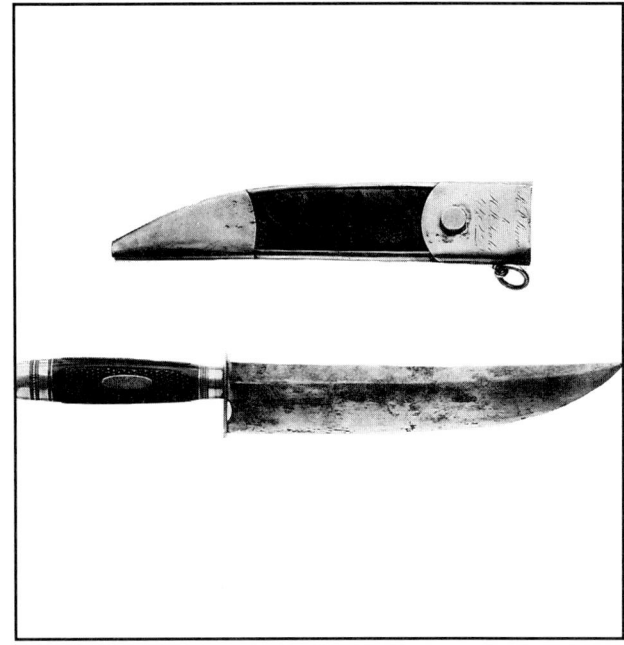

James Bowie's knife. It is on display inside the Alamo.

Alabama, Travis taught school and practiced law before going to Texas in 1831. He practiced law in Texas, too, and, being adventurous, became involved in the Texas colonists' early struggles for independence.

Davy Crockett, even then a well-known hunter, scout, and soldier, had been defeated in Tennessee for re-election to Congress. In 1835, looking for a new place to seek his fortune, he put on his buckskins and fur cap, picked up his rifle, called Old Betsy, and headed for Texas. And while he was at it, he might help the people of Texas. He had heard about their skirmishes with the

William Barret Travis

Davy Crockett

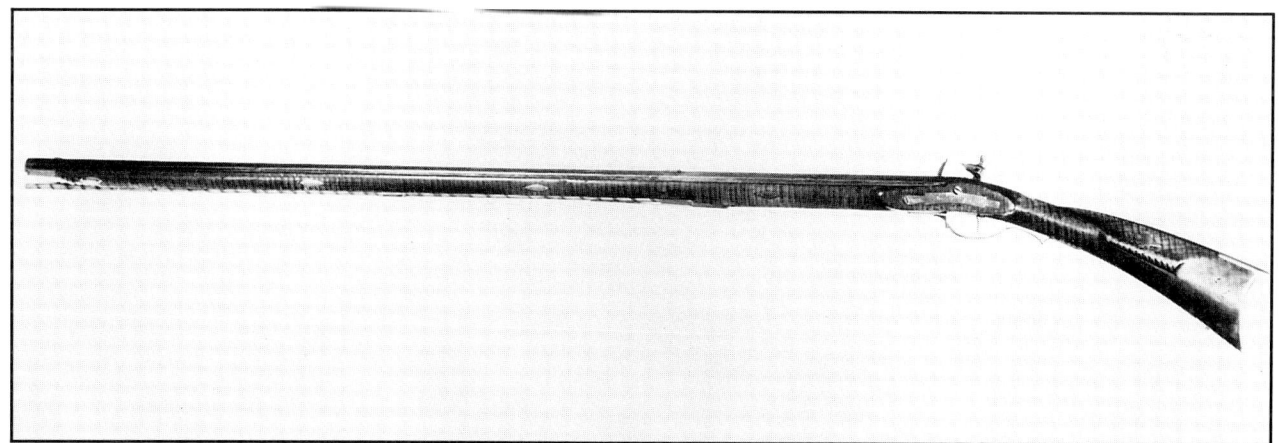
Davy Crockett's rifle. He called it "Old Betsy."

natives and about the Battle of Béxar. Arriving in Nacogdoches, 120 miles from San Antonio de Béxar, Crockett helped organize the Tennessee Company of Mounted Volunteers. When rumors came that Santa Anna was marching north to crush the Texans, Crockett and his volunteers headed south. They arrived at the Alamo on February 8.

Crockett's arrival at the Alamo did more than add manpower to the Texan defense. Crockett also lifted the men's spirits by playing his fiddle and telling the tall tales of adventure that had already made him famous. And he inspired the others at the Alamo when he boldly announced to Travis, "Colonel, just give me my place to defend, and me and my Tennessee boys will do it."

The other men who came to the Alamo were either soldiers in the Texan colonial army or ordinary volunteers, but all had extraordinary courage and determination. Some had fought in the Battle of Béxar, whose victory had only further fanned the flames of their desire for freedom. Most had come to this wild country just to acquire land and make homes for their families. Now they dreamed of a Texas Republic.

They were joined by some Texans of Spanish and Mexican descent, people who also had grown tired of

General Antonio López de Santa Anna

The Alamo as it appeared to the Mexican troops during the 13 day siege and final battle

Mexico's intolerable decrees and injustices. Also present at the Alamo were the families of two of the fort's defenders and a few of their servants.

The man stirring these Texas patriots to such bravery and determination was the president of Mexico, Santa Anna. As Mexico's leader, he was resolved to defend his territory. The Texans' disgracing of General Cos in the Battle of Béxar had been the last straw. Santa Anna quickly assembled about 6,000 troops and prepared to head north. On January 26, 1836, the powerful—as well as vain and ostentatious—president buckled on his jeweled sword valued at $7,000, mounted his gold-trimmed saddle, and began the month-long march to San Antonio de Béxar.

4
The Battle of the Alamo

Day 1. Tuesday, February 23, 1836

Daniel William Cloud, a volunteer originally from Kentucky, stood guard that morning, high in the bell tower of the San Fernando Church. It made a good lookout point. The church, across the San Antonio River and a short distance from the Alamo, was the highest building in the village of San Antonio de Béxar.

With eyes trained on an empty horizon, Cloud may have passed the time by thinking about his mother back in Kentucky or about St. Louis, where he had planned to practice law. But the opportunities seemed greater in this new territory, so he had come to Texas. Now he found himself staring out over its barren, flat, and cactus-dotted landscape. Was the rumor true? Was Santa Anna really planning to crush the Texans?

Little time was given him to wonder. With the sudden rumble of horses' hoofs, Cloud's peaceful watch was ended. Where just moments before the land had been clear and empty, it now was swarming with a sea of soldiers, the horizon ablaze with flashes made by the sun reflecting on sabers, lances, and helmets. Cloud grabbed the bell rope and frantically rang to alert the town. Santa Anna was coming.

Colonel Travis immediately ordered the small force of volunteers and soldiers who were staying in the town to go to the Alamo where they would make their stand for freedom. Mrs. Susanna Dickinson, the wife of one of the volunteers, her baby, and a handful of other people also rushed to the Alamo. In the village, some of the people fled and some hid, while others just awaited the outcome.

Outside the fort, Santa Anna lost no time in preparing for the attack. First he sent a courier to the fort demanding that the Texans surrender. Travis's answer was to fire a cannon. There would be no laying down of arms by these determined Texans. Then, from the same church tower where Daniel Cloud had stood just hours before, Santa Anna hoisted a blood-red flag, a sign that no quarter—no mercy—would be shown. All the men in the Alamo understood what that meant, that there would be no survivors. Should there be any lingering doubts about his intentions, Santa Anna also had his buglers play the dreaded tune, "Deguello," an ancient Moorish melody that announces the cutting of throats.

Day 2. Wednesday, February 24

Colonel Travis, only 26 years of age, assumed full command of the Alamo when Jim Bowie collapsed from pneumonia. Desperate for help, Travis sent urgent appeals to troops in other parts of Texas. The letters were carried at night by messengers who bravely dashed on horseback through showers of Mexican bullets.

Day 3. Thursday, February 25

While it was still dark, Santa Anna moved his army nearer the Alamo. He ordered his men to open fire from across the river, but his cannon were too far away for their shells to hurt anyone inside the Alamo. The Texans had a momentary victory: they shot back, killing two Mexicans and wounding six others. Travis sent another plea for help, this one to General Sam Houston, commander of the Texas colonial army.

Day 4. Friday, February 26

The men in the Alamo were chilled by the piercing winter wind. Gunfire was exchanged all day, and the Mexicans attempted to divert the irrigation system that supplied water to the Alamo. Crockett's Old Betsy kept finding its mark, felling any Mexicans who ventured too near the fort. Inside the Alamo, the defenders managed to avoid any casualties. By now it was clear to Santa Anna that more than a show of strength was needed to take the Alamo. It would take a full assault.

Day 5. Saturday, February 27

The weather continued to be cold and windy. Because of the continual Mexican gunfire, sleep was impossible for the small group of men inside the Alamo. Mexican troops tried again—but failed—to cut off the fort's water supply. The defenders of the Alamo were sure that help would arrive at any moment even though none had come so far. Colonel Travis sent a messenger to Colonel Fannin at Goliad with yet another plea for help.

Santa Anna ordered his musicians to play during the evening and night hours. At first the men inside the fort enjoyed the music, but later, as Santa Anna had calculated, the music became distressing as it kept the exhausted men awake.

Day 6. Sunday, February 28

A steady drizzle, a wintry wind, little rest, and meager food made the day miserable for the men inside the Alamo. While Santa Anna's forces continued shelling the fort, Davy Crockett provided some diversion to the troops by playing his fiddle. He was joined by another volunteer—John McGregor by name—a Texas colonist originally from Scotland, who played his bagpipes. The men in the Alamo needed some respite. It was becoming more obvious that reinforcements might never arrive, or at least not in enough time to help the men.

Day 7. Monday, February 29

Mexican troops moved closer to the Alamo. Though the Texans' gunpowder and cannon balls were fast disappearing, the men did not lose their fighting spirit. But if the Texans were brave, so were the Mexicans. They, too, had to face the chance of death even though they greatly outnumbered the poorly armed Texans.

Day 8. Tuesday, March 1

At 3:00 a.m., the men in the Alamo were encouraged by the arrival of 32 volunteers—men and boys—from the town of Gonzales. The men reported having heard rumors that 400 more troops were coming. Encouraged, the men continued firing their dwindling supply of cannon balls at Santa Anna's headquarters located across the plaza in front of the Alamo.

Day 9. Wednesday, March 2

Mexican cannon boomed all day, but the men inside the fort were still rejoicing that help had arrived and that there still was time for more to come.

Day 10. Thursday, March 3

Mexican battalions arrived to reinforce Santa Anna's army. Travis's messenger to Goliad returned alone, dodging bullets as he rode back through enemy lines. He sadly reported that no help would be coming. Goliad itself was being attacked. Santa Anna now had the Alamo surrounded after massing his infantry, moving up his artillery, and backing up those forces with cavalry.

Day 11. Friday, March 4

Santa Anna's army continued closing in on the Alamo. The men inside, with little ammunition left, used some of it to keep up their defense. They'd save the rest for the final struggle, which they knew lay just ahead.

Day 12. Saturday, March 5

Firing on the Alamo continued during the morning but let up in the afternoon. Then Santa Anna gave final orders: the Mexican army would storm the Alamo. Inside the fort, Colonel Travis assembled his men, realizing that

Travis drawing the line across the ground. "If you will stay and die with me, step across the line." Bowie asked to be carried across.

the defense of the Alamo could not hold out much longer. He told them what they themselves already must have known in their hearts—that there was no hope of help coming, and that they had three choices: to surrender, to try to escape, or to stay and fight. He pulled out his sword and drew a line across the ground in the Alamo's courtyard. "If you will stay and die with me, step across the line," he said.

One by one, the men began stepping across. Colonel Bowie, by now gravely ill, asked to be carried across on his cot. Only one man refused, choosing instead to escape over a wall.

Evening fell. Knowing that he and his men would soon be facing the final fight, Colonel Travis went to the part of the fort where Mrs. Dickinson was staying with her baby girl. Mrs. Dickinson had come to the fort to be with her beloved husband and to nurse wounded soldiers. Travis knelt by the baby and placed a string around the child's neck. It held a beautiful cat's eye stone ring. "I want Angelina to have this," he told Mrs. Dickinson. The ring was Travis's most treasured possession.

Day 13. Sunday, March 6

The Texans, hungry and collapsed with exhaustion, slept in the near-freezing temperature until a bugle blast suddenly awakened them before dawn. "The Mexicans are upon us!" their sentry yelled.

Four columns of Mexican soldiers were surging toward the fort. Deadly rounds of fire from the men in the Alamo stopped the first Mexican assault, but not without cost to the Texans. Colonel Travis died while defending the Alamo's north wall. Still, the Texans kept their positions, holding off the Mexicans two more times.

All the while, a Mexican bugler again played the menacing notes of "Deguello," signalling no mercy. Santa Anna then sent in reinforcements, who scaled ladders up the sides of the fort, slashing Texans with bayonets even as they climbed. The Texans in return clubbed the climbing Mexicans and shoved ladders away from the walls to the ground. At the same time, other Mexican soldiers were smashing two openings in the fort's walls.

Once the Mexicans were inside, hand-to-hand combat took place amidst the deafening fire of guns and the flash of bayonets. When the Texans ran out of ammunition, they used their rifles as clubs, swinging until their last man was dead.

The final struggle was brief. By 6:30 a.m., the Battle of the Alamo was over. Davy Crockett was dead, Old Betsy at his side, and Jim Bowie lay dead on his cot. His guns, too, were empty and his famous knife red with enemy blood. All 188 defenders of the Alamo had given their lives. And not only Texan colonists had died defending the fort. One fighter was a Mexican who supported the Texan cause against Mexican tyranny. Another sympathetic Mexican volunteer had brought his wife and four children to the Alamo by cover of night before giving his life in the struggle. His widow and children survived,

"Fall of the Alamo"

along with Mrs. Dickinson, Angelina, and the handful of other non-combatants who had taken refuge in the fort. Santa Anna spared their lives.

The Mexican leader had accomplished his goal. He had defended his land and won. But in so doing, he, too, paid dearly. He had lost an estimated 1,600 soldiers. "Another such victory and we are ruined," one of his officers is reported to have said. His words were prophetic.

5
A Brief Mexican Victory

Having taken the Alamo, the Mexicans summoned the women and children still hidden in it. Mrs. Dickinson and her baby, the only non-Mexicans, were brought before Santa Anna. "Go tell your Texan rebels what happened to those who dared to oppose me," he said to Mrs. Dickinson. "And tell them Santa Anna is coming."

Mrs. Dickinson took Angelina and hastened to General Sam Houston. As Mrs. Dickinson sobbed out the story of the Alamo, he consoled her, reassuring her that it had been impossible to get troops to the Alamo and that the bitter struggle had helped to slow Santa Anna's progress. The defense of the Alamo had given Houston time to gather his forces for the fight ahead.

And there would be fighting ahead. After their victory at the Alamo, the Mexicans set out to put a complete end to the Texas revolt. Three weeks after the fall of the fort, Santa Anna was in Goliad, where he massacred more than 300 prisoners he had taken in the siege of the town. But the Texans kept up the fight, now even more inspired by the battle cries, "Remember the Alamo" and "Remember Goliad."

"Surrender of Santa Anna"

In April, only 46 days after the Alamo fell, the enemies met again, this time in San Jacinto, the site of today's Houston, Texas. General Houston's forces of fewer than 800 Texans had come to camp near Santa Anna's army of 1,300 men. The Texans were able to take the overconfident Mexicans by surprise. The Battle of San Jacinto lasted only 18 minutes and brought death to 630 Mexicans. Houston captured Santa Anna and forced him to sign a treaty granting independence to Texas. After desperate struggles and painful losses, victory at last belonged to the Texans.

Texas became an independent republic, with Sam Houston elected as its first president and San Antonio—as it came simply to be called—its largest city. In 1845, just short of ten years after the Battle of the Alamo, Texas was admitted to the United States as the 28th state of the Union. It had come a long way since Stephen Austin's group of pioneer families had first set foot on Texas soil. It had come a long way since the valiant stand of the men of the Alamo.

6
San Antonio Today

Much time has passed since the Alamo fell and Texas gained its independence. Since then, San Antonio has grown to be America's tenth largest city and a blend of many cultures. The largest part of the city's million-plus population is of Mexican or Spanish descent. Among other significant groups that have helped settle and still live in the city are people of German, Irish, French, Italian, Greek, and African descent. These numerous groups daily mesh age-old traditions with new outlooks, making San Antonio a colorful and lively place to be.

San Antonio is located on the rolling plains of south-central Texas, about 140 miles from the Mexican border. It lies on the San Antonio River, which meanders through the heart of the city in a large horseshoe curve. The area has relatively mild winters, hot summers, and a dry climate that gives its citizens 300 days a year of blue and sunny skies. San Antonio is an important commercial and cultural center, and it is one of the nation's largest military centers. It is also the financial hub of the vast outlying agricultural and ranching areas. A wide range of manufacturing companies make their home in San

The Alamo at night

Antonio, producing everything from airplane parts to clothing. Medical and scientific research facilities are another San Antonio specialty.

But it is San Antonio's history and cultural life that make the city so unique. Let's visit some of San Antonio's sites and drop in on some of its many festivals.

7
A Visit to San Antonio

As you might have guessed, the Alamo is the most visited spot in San Antonio. Located near the San Antonio River in the heart of the city, the large mission compound is surrounded by an adobe wall. It has beautiful gardens and grounds. The Chapel is all that remains of the original mission buildings. Constructed of tan sandstone, the Chapel is worth a return trip at night when lights flood the Chapel, giving it a breathtaking golden glow. Next to the Chapel is the Long Barrack Museum and Library. The original Long Barrack had been a long narrow room where priests lived when the mission was active. The museum displays items from both Texas and Alamo history.

Near the Alamo is the IMAX Theater where visitors can see "Alamo—the Price of Freedom," a 45-minute film that tells the story of the fort's defenders. The screen in this theater is huge—six stories tall—and comes with a special sound system that puts you right into the middle of the action. Hold your hat! The cannon balls will whiz over your head, and horses' hoofs will thunder all around you.

River Walk

   The tree-lined, flower-studded *Paseo del Rio*, better known as the River Walk, is in the heart of downtown along the banks of the peaceful and winding San Antonio River. Shops line the way, and little sidewalk cafes offer food and entertainment. Mariachi (mah-ree-AH-chee) singers often serenade you as you eat. Mariachi is a type of Mexican folk music.

   Further along the River Walk you'll come to the Arneson River Theater, where you can see a play or hear just about any kind of concert. Be prepared for a surprise. The stage and audience of this outdoor theater are separated by the river! Spectators sit on grassy steps on one side of the river while the performance takes place on the other side.

Open-air barges float along the river. Visitors can ride on them and learn more about the city. It's an interesting ride whatever time of day you go, but it's especially scenic at night when city lights dance in reflection on the river's water. Other unique and pleasant ways to move around the city are open-air wooden trolleys and horse-drawn carriages.

As you continue along the River Walk, you'll come to *La Villita*, which means "little village" in Spanish. It's the site of the original San Antonio settlement that grew up around the first Mission San Antonio de Valero, the Alamo. The village has old brick- and tile-paved streets and restored stone houses where local artists and craftsworkers demonstrate and sell their works.

A visit to the Institute of Texan Cultures is a must. Through words, music, clothing, tools, and toys, it brings to life the story of some 30 cultural groups that have settled in Texas. Many exhibits feature a hands-on approach. Sit in front of a *tipi*—a Native American tent—while a guide tells you what life was like in a native village. In the Anglo-American section, pick the seeds from a cotton boll, or pod, and learn about the first American

Institute of Texan Cultures

cowboys, called *vaqueros*, from a Spanish word meaning "buckaroo." In the Institute's outdoor exhibit, explore life in rural Texas by visiting a one-room schoolhouse, a frontier fort headquarters, and a Texas adobe house. It's easy to see why nearly half a million people visit the Institute each year.

A stone's throw away is another of San Antonio's famous downtown sites, HemisFair Park, home of the world's fair held in 1968 to celebrate San Antonio's 250th birthday. The 750-foot Tower of the Americas is located there. From an observation deck at the top of the tower, you get a fantastic panoramic view of the city and see its landscape fade into the distant Texas hill country.

HemisFair Park with the Tower of the Americas in the background

San Antonio is the home not only of the Alamo but of four other historic 18th-century missions. They make up America's most complete Spanish colonial mission complex. The missions, still active churches, are outstanding examples of Spanish architecture and show how mission compounds were laid out.

If you enjoy museum-hopping, San Antonio is the perfect city for you. Its museums cover a huge variety of subjects. The Witte Museum has examples of natural history from Texas as well as the rest of the world. Take your pick of exhibits ranging from Texas frontier clothing to the animals of Texas, going all the way back to the dinosaurs that roamed the state 65 million years ago!

The Museum of Art has a great collection of Mexican folk art as well as ancient South American art going back to days before the Spanish arrived in the New World. The McNay Museum displays new Mexican arts and crafts as well as masterpieces from around the world.

For the best of fashion—Mexican folk fashion, that is—the Museum of Mexican Dress features folk dress and costumes from all over Mexico, one of Texas's strongest cultural ties.

Another good example of San Antonio's varied ethnic mix is the King William Historic District. The whole neighborhood is a museum of beautiful Victorian houses built by San Antonio's early German settlers, many of whom were prosperous businessmen.

Ready for some good old-fashioned playtime? The Memory Lane Museum of Dolls and Toys features thousands of dolls and toys that go back as far as the 1800s. And the Hertzberg Circus Collection is a treasure for children and adults alike. It displays more than 20,000 circus items from hundreds of years ago up to the present. Included is a miniature circus complete with side show, big top, animals, and performers. Don't miss the tiny coach of a truly tiny person, Tom Thumb.

Many visitors to San Antonio enjoy seeing one of the area's several military bases. Lackland Air Force Base is popular—it's called "home" by practically anyone who has ever served in the U.S. Air Force. The base is huge and has many fine displays, including a large aircraft exhibit and a Museum of Air Force History and Tradition.

The Fort Sam Houston Museum takes you back further in time. It shows the history of Fort Sam from its beginnings in 1845 to the present. You'll see buttons, uniforms, firearms, artillery, and photos as well as the fort's Army Medical Museum, representing more than 200 years of military medical history.

For a trip back to the Old West, the Pioneer, Trail Drivers, and Texas Rangers Museum displays saddles, badges, weapons, and other items from frontier days.

Calling all animal lovers!—or anyone who'd like to take an outdoor break. The San Antonio Zoo has a population of nearly 4,000 animals displayed in family groups and settings that resemble their natural habitats. It's only one of four zoos in the United States to have koalas, and it also offers an endangered whooping crane and a baboon island. You can hop a boat ride in the Children's Zoo. Another place for animal lovers is the Natural Bridge

Killer whale Baby Shamu jumps with her mother and father at the Sea World of Texas

Wildlife Ranch, not far from San Antonio. You travel along roads in a car and get to see—and feed—65 varieties of animals that come up to your car. You'll get a real close-up of the huge horns of a Texas longhorn steer. To see even more animals—marine animals, that is—Sea World of Texas, the world's largest marine-life park, is a fascinating stop. Be sure to catch the stars, Shamu and Baby Shamu, killer whales that put on a great show in a special pool of their own.

Time to rest your feet a bit? And these are only some of the many places to see in this memorable city. As soon as you're ready, let's drop in on some of San Antonio's many festivals.

8
A City of Fiestas

An exciting treat is in store for you if you're in San Antonio during any of its festivals, or *fiestas*—and the chances for that are good. There are plenty of them all through the year.

San Antonio, being a focal point of Texas history, has many festivals honoring the past. The biggest celebration of the year is April's ten-day Fiesta San Antonio, commemorating Texas' independence from Mexico. Magnificent parades, street parties, sporting events, music, art, and a dazzling procession of illuminated barges on the river are but a few highlights of this special event.

In March—the anniversary of the Battle of the Alamo—the people of San Antonio definitely "Remember the Alamo." On Alamo Memorial Day, ceremonies take place in the old mission/fort, which has become known as the "cradle of Texas liberty." Another special Alamo event is held in March by the Irish people of San Antonio, who have long been an important part of the community. In March not only do the Irish celebrate their traditional St. Patrick's Day, they also commemorate the defenders of the Alamo in a special wreath-laying ceremony. Among

Fiesta River Parade

the heroes of the Alamo were men of Irish descent, including 12 men born in Ireland.

May's *Cinco de Mayo*—the Fifth of May—marks another of the independence days that San Antonio commemorates. Six flags have flown over Texas during its history—the flags of Spain, France, Mexico, the Republic of Texas, the Confederate States of America, and the United States. Cinco de Mayo commemorates Mexico's independence from France. And in September there's another independence day—*Diez y Seis de Septiembre*—the Sixteenth of September—recalling Mexican independence from Spain. The event, which takes place along the San Antonio River and at *La Villita*, the city's oldest settlement, is filled with much festivity and music, as are all the other independence days.

St. Patrick's Day at Arneson River Theater

Speaking of music, each year special tributes are paid to the music that is uniquely Southwestern. May brings the Tejano Conjunto (tay-HAHN-oh kun-HOON-toe) Festival, dedicated to the truly authentic music born in South Texas from a mixture of Mexican and German influences. The nation's top *conjuntos* perform, and people can learn more about this vocal and instrumental music. November brings the Troubador Festival. It celebrates mariachi music and features some of the best mariachi groups performing this distinctive type of Mexican folk music.

But music is only one aspect of San Antonio's "melting pot" culture. With an ethnic heritage as rich as San Antonio's, there are many different people and traditions to celebrate. A real cultural explosion takes place in early August—the annual Texas Folklife Festival, a celebration of the state's 30 cultures. The four-day event is a huge sampling of everything ethnic—from food, dance, and music to costume, games, and art. Talk about extravaganzas...

October is another month that pays tribute to the city's cultural mix. Three different festivals honor three different groups that have long been important parts of San Antonio life: the Germans, the Greeks, and the African and Caribbean communities. Count on a lot of fun, fabulous food, and lively music at these ethnic fiestas.

And listen up now, pardner. Do you think San Antonio would be complete without a good slice of the Old West? Not a chance, so don't miss the 12-day Stock Show and Rodeo in February, a most appropriate tribute to bygone western days as well as the huge ranching and farming industry in today's Texas. This bronco-busting, lasso-snaring, showdown hoe-down is a mighty heap o' fun!

After a whole year of such lavish celebrations, San Antonio also closes the year with plenty of sparkle. If San Antonio has been called the City of Fiestas, it could just as easily be named the City of Lights—especially during the Christmas season. The sparkling begins with the Lighting and Holiday River Parade at the end of Novem-

Las Posadas

ber, when no fewer than 70,000 lights decorate bridges, buildings, and trees as well as the boats on the river. A highlight is the parade of decorated barges that plies its way down the gracefully curving river, casting beautiful colored reflections of light on the water. There are even more lights when the *Fiesta de las Luminaries*—the Festival of Lights—is held every weekend in December. The occasion is marked by the lighting of thousands of candles on the River Walk. And the River Walk is the center of another important holiday festival, *Las Posadas*—the Inns. It is a ceremony of song and—yes, more light, candlelight—which re-enacts the Holy Family's search for an inn. A procession, singing traditional songs and hymns, winds along the Walk until it reaches *La Villita*, where the clay figure of the infant Jesus is placed in a Nativity scene.

    The holiday spirit goes on and on, continuing with *Fiestas Navidenas*—Christmas Holidays. It features the blessing of pets, a visit from the Southwest's version of St. Nick—Pancho Claus!— and piñata parties for children, where they take turns trying to crack open fanciful creations filled with candy and other goodies. The holiday season even spills over into January, when *Los Pastores— The Shepherds—*is performed. It's a centuries-old Christmas play in which the forces of evil try—and fail—to keep the shepherds from going to Bethlehem to visit the Christ Child. The play is given at San Antonio's Mission of San Jose, a relic in its own right.

    Do you think you'll run out of things to do and see in San Antonio? Slim chance. This city is the home of far more than the Alamo. It's a city bursting with much more history and with just as much culture and fun. San Antonio is a memorable place to spend memorable time.

Index

Air Force 39
Alamo
  Battle of 5, 26, 30, 41
  Mexicans at 16, 26
  name 9
  Texans at 16, 19, 20, 22, 25, 26
  today 5
Alamo de Parras 9
Austin, Stephen 11, 30
Béxar 7
  Battle of 12, 13, 16, 17
Bowie, Jim 13, 14, 20, 24, 26
Christmas 12, 44, 46
Cloud, Daniel William 18, 19
Confederate States of America 42
Cos, Martín Perfecto de 11, 12, 13, 17
cottonwood trees 6, 9
Crockett, Davy 4, 14, 15, 16, 20, 21, 26
"Deguello" 19, 26
Dickinson, Susanna 19, 25, 27, 28
Fannin, Colonel 21
Gonzales 22
HemisFair Park 36, 37
Hertzberg Circus Collection 38
Houston, General Sam 20, 28, 29, 30
Houston, Texas 29
Institute of Texan Cultures 35, 36
Jameson, Green B. 13
King William Historic District 38
La Villita 35, 42, 46
Long Barrack 33
Los Pastores 46
McGregor, John 22

Mexico
  culture 11, 38
  independence from Spain 4, 9, 42
  military 5, 31, 39
  missions 5, 6, 7, 8, 9, 33, 35, 37, 41, 46
  museums 33, 37, 38, 39
Native Americans 7, 8, 35
Natural Bridge Wildlife Ranch 39-40
Paseo del Rio 34
Presidio de San Antonio de Béxar 7
"Remember the Alamo" 28, 41
River Walk 34-35, 45
rodeo 44
San Antonio
  climate 31
  culture 31, 32, 38, 43
  early history 5, 7, 10, 30
  festivals 41-46
  population 31
  today 31-32
San Antonio de Béxar 4, 8, 10, 13, 16, 17, 18
San Antonio River 6, 7, 18, 31, 33, 34, 42
San Fernando Church 18
San Jacinto, Battle of 29
Santa Anna, Antonio López de 4, 9, 11, 12, 13, 16, 17, 18, 19, 20, 21, 22, 23, 26, 27, 28, 29
Spain 4, 5, 9, 42
  and Mexico 4, 9, 42
  missions 5
  provincial government 8
Téran-Damián, Domingo de Manzanet 6

Texas
  frontier 4, 10
  independence 11, 13, 14, 30, 31, 41
  natural history 37
  Republic 16, 30, 42
  settlement 10-11
  terrain 31, 36
  territory 4, 9
Travis, Colonel William Barret 13, 14, 15, 16, 19, 20, 21, 23-25
Valero, Marquis of 6
vaqueros 36
zoos 39